DOGS SET IV

Bulldogs

Cari Meister
ABDO Publishing Company

visit us at
www.abdopub.com

Published by ABDO Publishing Company, 4940 Viking Drive, Suite 622, Edina,
Minnesota 55435. Copyright © 2001 by Abdo Consulting Group, Inc. International
copyrights reserved in all countries. No part of this book may be reproduced in any form
without written permission from the publisher.

Printed in the United States.

Cover Photo: Ron Kimball Studios
Interior Photos: Ron Kimball Studios (pages 5, 7, 9, 13, 15, 17, 21), AP/Wideworld
    (pages 11, 19)

Editors: Bob Italia, Tamara L. Britton, Kate A. Furlong, Christine Fournier
Art Direction: Neil Klinepier

Library of Congress Cataloging-in-Publication Data

Meister, Cari.
    Bulldogs / Cari Meister.
        p. cm. -- (Dogs. Set IV)
    Includes bibliographical references (p.).
    ISBN 1-57765-476-5
        1. Bulldog--Juvenile literature. [1. Bulldog. 2. Dogs. 3. Pets.] I. Title.

SF429.B85 M38 2001
636.72--dc21

                                                                    00-045384

Contents

The Dog Family

If you watch a wolf cub playing, it may remind you of a dog. This is because dogs and wolves are closely related.

Dogs and wolves belong to the same **family**, called Canidae. There are 37 different **species** in the canid family. Foxes and jackals are also members of the canid family.

Members of the canid family share many of the same **traits**. They have similar body shapes and functions. Both dogs and wolves are pack animals. This means they like to live in a big group.

Thousands of years ago, people tamed wild dogs. Today, millions of people all over the world have pet dogs. There are over 400 different **breeds** of dogs. One of the most popular is the bulldog.

Bulldogs have an excellent sense of smell.

Bulldogs

Bulldogs were developed hundreds of years ago in England. Early bulldogs were bred for strength and fierceness. Bulldog owners wanted brave, tough dogs to use in bullbaiting.

Bullbaiting is a sport in which a bulldog bites and holds onto a bull's nose. People bet money on which dogs could hold on the longest.

Bullbaiting was outlawed in 1835. After that, the bulldog nearly became **extinct**. But people who liked the bulldog saved it. They bred bulldogs that were not fierce fighting dogs. Today, bulldogs are one of the friendliest dog breeds.

Opposite page: The fierce-looking bulldog is actually friendly.

What They're Like

Bulldogs are strong, quiet dogs. They also can be **stubborn**. Most bulldogs are family pets. But some people show their bulldogs in dog shows.

Bulldogs are usually good around other dogs. They can enjoy the company of cats, too. But if a bulldog is not used to being around other animals, it may become protective of its toys, owner, and food.

Be careful when introducing adult bulldogs to other animals. You will never know for sure how they will act. Make sure the animals get along before you leave them alone together. And always have separate food and water dishes for each animal.

Bulldogs can be quite protective of their territory.

Coat and Color

Bulldogs have smooth, short coats. Their coats contain special oils that keep dirt off their bodies. Bulldogs do not need to be bathed often. Too many baths will wash away the oils. Then their coats will be dry and dirty.

Bulldogs come in many colors. They can be white, red, or tan. Bulldogs can also be piebald. Piebald dogs are white with patches of another color. Some bulldogs are brindle. These dogs are streaked with many shades of color.

Bulldogs have very wrinkly faces. Bulldog owners need to take special care to keep their bulldog's face clean. Owners should check between the wrinkles daily. If the skin between the folds is damp, put a little **talcum** powder on it. This will help dry the area out and prevent **infection**.

This bulldog has a brindle coat.

Size

Bulldogs are short, sturdy dogs. They stand between 13 and 15 inches (34-38 cm) tall at the shoulder. Bulldogs have very wide, strong shoulders. Male bulldogs weigh about 50 pounds (23 kg). Female bulldogs weigh about 40 pounds (18 kg).

Bulldogs have large heads with flat foreheads and blunt **muzzles**. They have large black noses. Their noses are also short and flat. This makes it hard for some bulldogs to breathe. Sometimes they wheeze or gulp air.

Bulldogs have a mean facial expression. Bulldogs have the nickname Sourmug. Bulldogs look this way because of how the bones in their face and jaw are set. But most bulldogs are very friendly.

Opposite page: The shape of their nose makes some bulldogs snore loudly!

Care

Bulldogs are easy to care for. They do not need much exercise. In fact, it is **dangerous** for a bulldog to get too much exercise.

Bulldogs should never be expected to run very far. They should only go for short walks a couple of times a day.

Never exercise a bulldog when it is hot or **humid**. Bulldogs get overheated and have a hard time breathing.

When bulldogs get too hot, they **pant**. This is how they cool their bodies. But if a bulldog pants too long, its throat may swell. Many bulldogs die from **heatstroke**.

It is a good idea to keep a bulldog in an air-conditioned home. Some owners have small wading pools in their yard for their bulldogs to sit in. But the pool can't be very full. Bulldogs cannot swim.

This bulldog is panting.

Feeding

Bulldogs should eat a meaty dog food twice a day. There are many types of dog food. It does not matter which kind you feed your bulldog, as long as it is **nutritionally** complete and your dog likes it.

Bulldog puppies need to eat more often than adult dogs. Before you take your puppy home, ask the breeder how often the puppy was fed. Find out what kind of food it ate. Follow the same diet for awhile. Then when the puppy is about six months old, begin feeding it two meals a day.

It is very important that bulldogs drink lots of water. This keeps them from getting overheated. Bulldogs should always have a big bowl of fresh water available.

Bulldog puppies eat several meals a day.

Things They Need

Bulldogs do best when they live indoors. They do poorly in very hot or very cold weather.

If your bulldog must be outside in the summer, make sure it has shade and lots of water. If your bulldog must be outside during winter, make sure there is a doghouse or other place to shelter it from the cold.

Bulldogs should have a yearly checkup with a **veterinarian**. A veterinarian can give them shots to prevent diseases like **distemper** and **rabies**.

Bulldogs are **stubborn**. They may not come when they are called. Bulldogs should be walked on a leash. That way, they will not wander off. In case your bulldog gets lost, make sure it has a dog tag with your phone number on it.

Opposite page: Choose a good, strong leash for your bulldog.

Puppies

Bulldog puppies have very large heads. This makes it hard for the mother bulldog to give birth. This is **dangerous** for the mother and the puppies. Sometimes, a **veterinarian** must help the mother dog have the puppies.

After the puppies are born, it is very important to keep them and their mother in a warm place. Bulldog puppies are bigger than lots of other puppies. They usually weigh 10 to 12 ounces (284-340 g). But like all puppies, bulldogs are helpless when they are born. They depend on their mother for everything.

Bulldog mothers can be clumsy. Sometimes, they accidentally sit or lay on their puppies. If your bulldog has puppies, check on them every hour or so to make sure no puppies are trapped!

A bulldog mother and her pup

Glossary

breed: a group of dogs that share the same appearance and characteristics.

dangerous: able to cause pain, injury, or harm.

distemper: a virus that dogs get. It is marked by breathing, stomach, and nerve problems.

extinct: something that no longer exists.

family: a group that scientists use to classify similar plants and animals. It ranks above a genus and below an order.

heatstroke: a condition marked by sweating, high body temperature, and fainting. It is caused by long exposure to high temperatures.

humid: moisture or dampness in the air.

infection: a sickness in people or animals caused by contact with germs.

muzzle: the jaws and nose of an animal; snout.

nutrition: important parts of a diet that all living things need to survive.

pant: to breathe heavily.

rabies: a sickness of warm-blooded animals that causes abnormal behavior, increases saliva, and usually leads to death.

species: a class or family of individuals having common traits and a common name.

stubborn: being headstrong and not giving in.

talcum: powder made from a soft, soapy-feeling mineral.
trait: a feature of a person or animal.
veterinarian: a person with medical training who cares for animals.

Internet Sites

The American Kennel Club
http://www.akc.org
Research your favorite breed at the official AKC site.

Bulldog Club of America
http://www.thebca.org
Read about the history of the bulldog and the standard of the breed. Learn about upcoming shows and see portraits of National Show winners.

Dog Owner's Guide - Online Magazine for Dog Owners
http://www.canismajor.com/dog/bulldog.html
Learn all about bulldog behavior, care, and history on this site for dog lovers.

Index